SEMINARY FLAW
AND SOLUTION

PASTOR DEFICIENCY

HENRY (HANK) LOYD COPELAND

authorHOUSE®

AuthorHouse™
1663 Liberty Drive
Bloomington, IN 47403
www.authorhouse.com
Phone: 1 (800) 839-8640

Published by AuthorHouse 06/01/2018

ISBN: 978-1-5462-4507-0 (sc)
ISBN: 978-1-5462-4506-3 (e)

Library of Congress Control Number: 2018906525

Print information available on the last page.

Any people depicted in stock imagery provided by Getty Images are models, and such images are being used for illustrative purposes only. Certain stock imagery © Getty Images.

This book is printed on acid-free paper.

CONTENTS

CONTENTS

DEDICATION

This book is dedicated to those church members who have experienced church management problems and recognized that one cannot escalate a problem to the 'top' and expect it to be resolved when the capability is not there. This can cause deep rooted dissatisfactions, frustrations, and can result in disappointment and anger. It is hoped that this book will: a) contribute toward reducing some causes of these dissatisfactions, and b) contribute to church growth both spiritually and in number.

This book is dedicated first and foremost to his late wife with respect, gratitude, and affection:

Amy Elsie Suther Copeland

Wife, Mother, Friend, and Angel

Children

    Amy Sue Wavra
    Bradley Clark Copeland
    Daniel Loyd Copeland

This book also is dedicated to those twenty-five (25) families who were members of the Media Ministries team for several years.

ACKNOWLEDGEMENT

The author acknowledges all those individuals who sincerely and steadfastly stuck to the poor management 'business as usual' philosophy that destroyed Media Ministries. If the author had not encountered this kind of poor management, this book would not have been written. One cannot escalate a problem to the 'top' and expect it to be resolved when the capability is not there.

The author also acknowledges The Holy Spirit as providing 'peace that passes all understanding'; turning the author's negative 'hurt' feelings into a positive.

FOREWORD

Colossians 3:17. "…do everything in the name of the Lord Jesus…"

It has been said that the greatest power in the world is the power to communicate with Almighty God. It is recommended that seminary leaders, seminary students, Pastors, and Lay leaders who read this book read it prayerfully and take its content to God in prayer for guidance. Above all, do not cast it aside as 'business as usual'.

The purpose of this book is to significantly improve church leadership; those who are seminary leaders, seminary students, Pastors, and Lay leaders. Leadership of the church, the Body of Christ on earth, is a very serious matter. As such, leadership should be most interested in improving its efficiency and effectiveness. Without knowing, many Pastors and Lay Leaders could further improve their vision and make significant positive changes in their management philosophy. Get rid of 'business as usual'. Yes; 'business as usual' requires less work and is much easier. 'Business as usual' requires minimal management capability. But, without realizing it, 'business as usual' is a deterrent to progress. Why is 'business as usual' happening? Leaders have not been given that portion of the educational foundation needed to most completely 'manage' a church. Seminaries can provide this needed foundation by adding a management course to their curriculum.

TESTIMONY

Media Ministries was founded by me during 2007; however, I did not know it. Over a period of seven years, the Holy Spirit guided me in small steps having me continually finance, design, build, staff, and operate Media Ministries. It touched many people including the operating personnel as they became a happy team getting to work with each other and seeing what the Holy Spirit was building. It became a real joy to see the results of the Holy Spirit's guidance. APPENDIX A presents Media Ministries Operating Plan and APPENDIX I presents Media Ministries History. Appendix I should be read at this point.

In 2015 the church assumed responsibility for Media Ministries; however, it was <u>in name only</u>. The 'business as usual' church leadership ignored the Operating Plan, and allowed Media Ministries to be destroyed (almost complete non-compliance with the Media Ministries Operating Plan). All of this invested time, talent, and money, as I saw it with my secular eyes, became of no value. Imagine the psychological impact of such a drastic change.

Initially, the feeling was deep hurt. Prayer in terms of "Thy will be done" was done in wonder. Why? Continual prayer led me to believe that the Holy Spirit did not want this kind of thing to happen and that He wants His church, The Body of Christ, managed much more efficiently and effectively by getting rid of business as usual and replacing it with much better management utilizing: leadership and planning, organizing, staffing, motivating, and controlling. The Holy Spirit provided me 'peace that passed all understanding'. The 'hurt' was gone, and instead of feeling and acting negatively, my thoughts became positive. In my looking at the BIG picture, and trying to figure out where to go from here, I believe the Holy Spirit wants me to apply my management knowledge and experience to better help the church by writing "Seminary Flaw". "Seminary Flaw" uses actual negative events to expose poor management and reveal the need for Seminaries to include a 'management' course, not just a leadership course, in their curriculum. This has a much broader scope than Media Ministries.

CHAPTER 1 – INTRODUCTION

MESSAGE TO CHURCH LEADERS
What are your preconceptions?
Do you have capability to change?
Are you open to changes?
Will your preconceptions stand in the way of improving
the efficiency and effectiveness of the church?

Instead of doubting everything that can be doubted, let us
rather doubt nothing until we are compelled to doubt.

PROBLEM STATEMENT

Sometime it is very difficult to get someone's attention, especially when they rarely, if ever, try to seek out constructive criticism or find ways to improve even though constructive criticism could lead to improvement. Why? Positively acting on constructive criticism could require change, and change is a challenge to business as usual. Also, the defense mechanism kicks in without understanding the depth of the constructive criticism; "We already have a management course in the curriculum; we call it 'leadership', the term 'management' implies hierarchy which implies dictatorship. The church is a relational organization." This appears to be the reason for 'leadership' education in contrast to 'management' education.

The not-for-profit churches are referred to as 'relational' and the for-profit businesses are referred to as 'hierarchical'. Both apply the basic functions of management included in business textbooks, namely,

- Planning
- Organizing
- Staffing
- Motivating
- Controlling

However, this book assumes, and rightly so, that church leadership needs to more fully learn: a) the full meaning of each of these functions, b) how to implement each of these functions, and c) and experience implementing each of these functions.

Why do churches use the relational technique? The answer is that the church is staffed with volunteers with exception of some paid employees, and directing is considered too harsh for volunteers. This is a major fundamental misunderstanding as to how the hierarchical philosophy is used. This misunderstanding can be largely due to having worked in only the church environment.

The following terminology can be used in appreciating the text in this book.

Leadership - A process of social influence in which a person can enlist the aid and support of others in the accomplishment of a task.

Management – A process in which a person 'can' enlist the aid and support of others in planning, organizing, staffing, motivating, and controlling in the accomplishment of a task.

The term 'leadership' places emphasis on 'social influence' whereas 'management' places emphasis on planning, organizing, staffing, motivating, and controlling. Both use 'social influence' in actual practice; however, the term 'leadership', as such, is not normally included as a basic function of management. It is both implied and included in other business courses. So, add 'leadership' to the basic functions of management for church application to achieve the objective that planning, organizing, staffing, motivating, and controlling will be equally emphasized in the course. Also, change the current 'leadership' course to 'management' course. **Thus, the basic functions of management become: leadership, planning, organizing, staffing, motivating, and controlling.**

The reader of this book who has theological education background most likely is both aware that 'leadership' is taught in seminaries, and has taken the course; however, it is apparent that 'leadership' education takes lower priority, as it should, to theological education. This is evidenced in worse case by making 'leadership' an elective. There also is an 'internship' course where the student works in a church for maybe a year part time. This is where the student is to get exposure to the actual functioning of a church. Neither of these is sufficiently intense as one of the theological courses. Not only is there a lack of intensity, but also, the content of a 'leadership' course is inadequate as compared to a 'management' course that covers the basic functions of management, namely, leadership, planning, organizing, staffing, motivating, and controlling. As a result, the student upon ordination is not prepared to effectively contribute using the basic functions of management. This can result in poor performance as noted in the cases included in this book. This poor performance can also result in churches not having written plans to accomplish what Seminaries have included, as the intent to be accomplished, in their mission statements. It is a fact that without 'management' education, a Pastor will be significantly less effective in applying theological education.

END OF PROBLEM STATEMENT

The main purpose of this book is to achieve the objective of getting Seminaries to include a management course that includes: leadership, planning, organizing, staffing, motivating, and controlling in their curriculum. The lack of a management course in the Seminary curriculum is a very serious flaw. Pastors need to recognize the need for and seek management training. This is highly evident as exposed in this book where there is so much poor management. Many churches seem to be satisfied with what they are doing and continue with 'business as usual'. The degree to which progress beyond 'business as usual' is understood depends on the depth of understanding how to implement the basic functions of management in the church. 'Business as usual' would say, and has said, at this point: "It's not worth it".

The extent to which the content of this book can be applied is significantly influenced by the size of the church. However, the fundamental principles of the basic functions of management apply independent of the size of the church. And, it should be noted here that no matter how hard a Pastor tries to grow a church, there are cases where almost nothing can become effective.

The term 'management' is used in this book to represent the ruling body of the individual church. The ruling body can be the Board of Deacons in one church, The Session including Elders in another church, etc. Organizations within this 'management' are referred to in this book as "Components' in contrast to "committees". The ruling body organizational structure including its Components is discussed further in Chapter 3 – Organizational Structure and Mechanical Management.

Some church leaders consider the term 'management' not applicable to the church because the church is mostly a volunteer organization and that the term 'management' implies a more hierarchical dictatorial concept. This does not have to be the case, especially in the church. Inclusion of 'leadership' in the management course should eliminate this concern. Church managers should make decisions and provide direction in such a way as to 'get the job done' without being a dictator and warranting negative criticism. It can be done. Personality is very important as well as true leadership capability.

The purpose of this book also is to be positive; to lift up or build up the church and not tear it down. **This book must be read with a positive attitude looking for what might improve church performance.** Improving implies change, and change for the better.

It is understood that the church as a whole is decreasing in membership. This is a case of some individual churches having a 'terminal disease' without knowing it. One church, and there are apparently more, membership has decreased by more than 50% relative to its peak, and not only is there no expressed serious concern, there is no plan to stop this decrease. The statistics are only casually reported to the congregation annually. In many cases, the cause of this problem is a combination of 'business as usual', lack of 'know how', and lack of in-depth knowledge of and dependence on The Holy Spirit. Membership in the church should be increasing and not decreasing.

The one big excuse for acceptance of decline in membership is that 'church membership is on the decline'. There are many reasons for such decline; however, this decline should be a challenge to church leadership. In other words, leadership should DO SOMETHING ABOUT IT. The church should not accept, in general, loss of membership, but should take advantage of anything that could grow the church. One thing that should be done is eliminate 'business as usual' since it is apparent that it is not working.

It is essential that Seminaries add a management course to their curriculum to be taught on campus and its satellites and in churches and their satellites for those Pastors and Lay leaders who are already leaders in churches. A Pastor should be both a church manager as well as a spiritual leader. Being a church manager does not imply that the Pastor should be a dictator. Being a church manager requires sensitivity and means by which to effectively lead without offending. Again, church managers should make decisions and provide direction in such a way as to 'get the job done' without being a dictator and warranting negative criticism. A Pastor must have vision and avoid ineffective "business as usual". Without management training, it is easy to not "rock the boat" and fall into the "business as usual" pitfall.

This book uses a true major negative event, namely the destruction of Media Ministries (See Appendix A – Media Ministries Operating Plan and Appendix I – Media Ministries History), caused by poor management, to contrast or emphasize the need for seminaries to include a management course in their curriculum. Appendix I should be read at this point.

Destruction of Media Ministries was an activity that was large enough to provide in-depth insight into management of the church. Many Pastors and congregations are operating in this type of environment, and do not have the education that could provide this in-depth insight. As a result, business as usual continues to exist, and a church, and there are many, that have great potential continue to decline in membership as well as not perform as they should perform.

The creation of Media Ministries took several years. As the scripture says, the Holy Spirit will give you no more to do than you are capable of doing. In this case, implementing the vision took: time, talent, personnel, and money. It is somewhat like founding a business. It progresses slowly in increments. Even though a detailed Operating Plan was prepared and distributed to key people, and meetings were held with these key people, no one really grasped the total scope. No one really had an in-depth appreciation. In other words, no one assumed responsibility for reading the Operating Plan and assuring continuation of Media Ministries as defined in the Operating Plan. Therefore, leadership, probably unintentionally, allowed lack of compliance with the Operating Plan through neglect or 'business as usual'. Also, none of the congregation read the Operating Plan, so the congregation can think Media Ministries still exists even though it exists in name only. Decisions were made that destroyed Media Ministries, and no one detected this in advance or as it was occurring, and no one intervened.

This book does not attempt to design the management course. This book provides case descriptions that form the basis for why the course should be included in the Seminary curriculum and some examples to avoid. This book also provides discussions and guidelines to use in implementing the basic functions of management used in church program management. Appendices, namely, planning, staffing, motivating and controlling, and others also are included. Here again, the term controlling must be done appropriately to 'get the job done' without being a dictator and warranting negative criticism. Again, inclusion of 'leadership' in the management course should eliminate this concern.

Also, the management course should include the preparation of plans to accomplish what Seminaries have included, as the intent to be accomplished, in their mission statements. Use the organization included in Chapter 3 Figure 1 as a model as if the plans were to be actually used by churches. These plans could be very helpful as models for churches if the plans were shared. Seminary encouragement for written plan sharing could be one significant source of information feedback that could reveal the need for Seminaries to include a management course in their curriculum.

CHAPTER 2 – CHURCH MANAGEMENT ENVIRONMENT

MESSAGE TO CHURCH LEADERS
What are your preconceptions?
Do you have capability to change?
Are you open to changes?
Will your preconceptions stand in the way of improving
the efficiency and effectiveness of the church?

Instead of doubting everything that can be doubted, let us
rather doubt nothing until we are compelled to doubt.

Many churches have no 'management environment'. They are virtually 100% spiritual, and this is considered most, if not all that is desired. However, the item that is missing is application of 'management' that could further expand effectiveness of its mission of carrying the gospel to the world. The central focus of every part of the church should be building up the church spiritually and carrying the gospel to all. **Leadership should see to it that membership recognize with emphasis that there are souls out there that must be saved, and DO SOMETHING ABOUT IT.** This cannot be accomplished efficiently and effectively without good management.

Seminaries are producing Pastors who have inadequate management knowledge. Apparently, it is expected that they will get that 'hands on' experience when they are ordained and become the Pastor of a church. This is a disservice to both Pastors and churches. Seminaries can solve this problem by providing a management course in their curriculum. A course that has a seminary student assigned to a church for a short period of time does not suffice.

In the 'long established' environment, such events as the destruction of Media Ministries can occur. The Pastor is not responsible, and the 'ruling body' as a whole is not responsible, and the Chairs of each Component of the 'ruling body' are not responsible. So, NOBODY IS RESPONSIBLE. Also, crudely speaking, NOBODY CARES.

There are many good things that can be said about the church; however, progress is not only continuing to do good things, but also abandoning the 'business as usual' philosophy. The result can be change that improves overall performance if there is 'know how' and desire.

Professionals who are members of the church including medical doctors, lawyers, and others who are well educated do not have the appropriate business education and experience that a seminary course could provide.

The following problem areas, not necessarily in order of importance, have been identified within one church that has tremendous potential; however, it does not have the management capability to capitalize on this potential.

These problem areas can be used to identify the source of problems as well as lead to corrective action.

PROBLEM AREAS & COMMENTS

1. Media Ministries destruction; the task was assumed by the church in name only without knowingly, and personnel who indicated that they would 'assume responsibility' for the task seemed to have had no intention to comply with the Operating Plan; ignored it. This destruction destroyed many tasks, one of which was a 'global ministry'.

Comment: Management should consider it important enough to be quite familiar with all tasks performed in the church. This should be particularly true when an operating plan exists detailing the tasks to be performed. It is obvious that this was not the case with Media Ministries. No one took steps to assure that Media Ministries continued to function. This poor performance reflects on **ALL** leaders in the church. Chapter 3 – Organizational Structure & Mechanical Management identifies the leaders as the Board and each of the Component Chairs. Each Chair should assume responsibility for contributing to the success not only of his/her Component but also for the entire Board by providing constructive criticism of each other Chair's plan and performance to plan. If this were the case, this destruction should not have occurred.

2. A newly assigned individual to take responsibility for a significant Component asks: "What am I supposed to do, invent the wheel – no plan or job description?" This occurred almost every year when there was a transition of Component assignments.

Comment: The Board should have a mission statement and its plan and each Component Chair should have its plan. A plan is a list of objectives in both broad and detailed terms. There must be enough detail for the church leaders to identify the individual tasks that can be both assigned to and performed by individuals. It should include procedures as to how to achieve the objectives. It should include staffing requirements. The plan not only guides Component performance by existing personnel but also provides guidance to newly incoming Component staff. In businesses there are tactical and strategic plans; tactical meaning near term and strategic meaning long term.

3. One person has significant influence in budget allocations and controls all budget expenditures.

Comment: Each Component should have its own budget and manage accordingly. Assigning a budget for each Component provides for: a) budget sensitivity, b) funds necessary to perform the task according to plan, and c) experience to be gained in managing within budget.

4. "I don't have the capability to do that."

Comment: This is a recruiting problem when there is no attempt to match the person's capability with the assigned task.

5. "I (Pastor) am not the director of management (ruling body); the 'ruling body' provides direction.

Comment: It is contrary to most organizations, to exist without one leader. The Board leader can introduce both efficiency and effectiveness in Board performance in such a way as to not be a dictator.

6. A Leader who is not a part of management has responsibility for a significant task, and needs support from management, but does not know to whom in management to ask for support.

Comment: There is a severe breakdown in communications when the leaders including Component Chairs do not know for what each other is responsible. In this case the leader needing support did not know his/her Component Chair, and vise-versa. The Chair should be sufficiently knowledgeable to recognize the need to provide support and work with the leader in providing it.

7. There are often visiting individuals who replace the Pastor in a worship service or visit one or more of the management Components. There is no

one who is their host. They arrive, and there is no one to welcome them or provide needed support.

Comment: The Component Chairs should have included in their Component plans the need for hosting as noted in APPENDIX B – Hosting and provide hosts from within their Component.

8. A newly assigned person to assume responsibility for Media Ministries makes a unilateral statement: "I am not going to do that!" even though the task is identified in the Operating Plan. This eliminated a major task. This occurred in several areas and continued occurring until many major task areas were eliminated.

Comment: This is both a severe: a) personnel problem and b) management problem. This type of problem could have been avoided if management had properly transferred the task.

9. A person responsible for a key task was asked to collect together in one place individual policy decisions made by management over the past years, and his response was: "that's not my job" even though the task could be accomplished at his leisure not to a schedule.

Comment: The Board plan should have included this task, and if it were in the plan, this problem would not have existed. Also, the entire church could be detrimentally affected if this problem is not resolved.

10. The Church Management System (CMS) database has a great deal of capability or 'tools' of management; however, it is used in a limited sense, and there is no policy governing what capability should and should not be used.

Comment: This is a severe management problem that reflects on the lack of management capability of recognizing and using available 'tools' of management.

11. "Well, we got that meeting over within an hour."

Comment: This is an attitude problem that should not exist if the Board Leader had the management education to function as noted in this book. Having a short meeting is more important than preparing, for example, Component plans that did not exist. Yes, meetings should be conducted efficiently, but there are many things that should be done.

12. Written policies were submitted properly for approval, but there was no response. Some of these were relative to member and non-member usage of facilities.

Comment: This could be negligence, lack of understanding the problem, or intentional avoidance. One non-member organization requested authorization to use facilities but just had to use facilities without receiving a response.

13. Key targets (goals) were set but no plan existed for accomplishment.

Comment: A plan must be prepared to provide the 'road map' to accomplish goals. Also, it is not enough to have a plan without some detail as to how to implement the plan.

14. The Pastor's desire for mission giving was 10% of the operating budget; however, only 6% to 7% was allocated.

Comment: This occurred during each of several years and became 'business as usual'. No plan was prepared to achieve this goal.

15. Members stop attending, and no one contacts them or even sends a card or letter: a) trying to find out why or, b) encouraging them to return.

Comment: Members just 'fade away'. This is one of many reasons membership is declining. There are cases that can be easily resolved, and there are cases that are very difficult to resolve. Also, the reason for the absence could be so profound that management can't handle it? If this is so, the church might have a deep rooted problem that needs attention.

16. Members stop pledging, and no one contacts them or sends a card or letter, other than a form letter, asking them to pledge each year. No one attempts to find out why.

Comment: Members just 'fade away'. This is one of many reasons membership is declining. There are cases that can be easily resolved, and there are cases that are very difficult to resolve. Also, the reason for the absence could be so profound that management can't handle it? If this is so, the church might have a deep rooted problem that needs attention.

17. Transition of leadership assignment from one leader to another leader results in loss of personnel contacts, especially relative to missionaries.

Comment: There is no plan for the existing Component personnel to introduce the incoming personnel to key missionaries. In this case, the missionaries just 'fade away'.

18. Subwoofers (sound speakers) introduce hum into the sound system when they are on. The solution was to disconnect them and forget trying to find a solution to the problem.

Comment: This is an example of eliminating the task in contrast to solving the problem. In other words, 'we don't need the subwoofers', which is either a lack of understanding of the sound system or a 'shallow' conclusion to take the easy way out.

19. One business executive of the church volunteered his secretary to make assignments for Media Ministries' personnel on a weekly basis. This involved assigning nine (9) volunteer personnel each week to perform different weekly tasks as outlined in the Media Ministries Operating Plan. Needed changes in assignments occurred almost every week. In summary, this was a significant task. The church member who assumed responsibility for Media Ministries, when the church assumed its responsibility, said: "I will make the assignments."

<u>Comment</u>: This was an indicator of the lack of how to manage personnel. There was no contact informing the secretary of this decision; it just happened.

20. Proposal to implement preparation of Operating Plan was rejected. Refer to APPENDIX E – Rejected Operating Plan Proposal.

Comment: This proposal was an attempt to implement use of some of the functions of management, namely plan preparation, by leadership. It was rejected most likely because of either: 1) a lack of training preparation of leadership before the proposal was presented, or 2) lack of leadership knowledge and appreciation of basic functions of management. It was just too much to absorb. It can be seen from this experience that management training is vital to the understanding and appreciation of the content of a good management course. In this case neither the Leader nor Chairs had such education. So, it has been said, "There is no need to escalate a problem to the top if capability is not there". Unfortunately, this rejection could be an indicator of the future of this church.

'Management' does not replace prayer.

Prayer is top priority. The topic of prayer should be a part of the management course. It is assumed that Seminaries equip Pastors spiritually and especially with prayer. However, the significance of prayer and the relationship of Pastors and Lay personnel to the basic functions of management and especially The Holy Spirit must be strongly emphasized. There must be **genuine** fervor – zeal, passion, intensity, earnestness, enthusiasm.

CHAPTER 3 – ORGANIZATIONAL STRUCTURE & MECHANCAL MANAGEMENT

MESSAGE TO CHURCH LEADERS
What are your preconceptions?
Do you have capability to change?
Are you open to changes?
Will your preconceptions stand in the way of improving
the efficiency and effectiveness of the church?

Instead of doubting everything that can be doubted, let us
rather doubt nothing until we are compelled to doubt.

An example organizational structure is shown in Figure 1. The term 'mechanical management' is used to describe relationships and actions taken within and between elements of the organizational structure. This is a team that should function efficiently and effectively in harmony. Organizational structure is referred to in this book as the "Leadership Board" and 'Board' will be used for short. The Board in some churches is called Board of Deacons, and the Board in other churches is called Session, and etc. Other churches might have different names for the Board. The Board is composed of Components. Components are top level areas of responsibility. This terminology is unique to this book. The Leader is in charge of the Board and a Chair is in charge of a Component. The Board as a whole is not considered the Leader in this book. There is only one Leader who is the Leader of the Board and this Leader is responsible for the performance of each Chair. This Leader provides guidance and direction to each Chair. This Leader is the senior pastor and should be a biblical scholar and a person who believes in and knows the need for good management and has the 'know how' to apply good management. Here again, this sounds 'harsh', but it does not have to be 'harsh'. A church can be properly led by a Pastor who has been educated in a management course provided by the seminary.

The Leader of the Board is a salaried professional ordained minister and has line authority over the Associate Leaders and the Chairs. The Leader's job description should include both spiritual and management. Associate Leaders are salaried professionals who have expertise in one or more church discipline and: a) perform their tasks within that discipline which is within the scope of one or more Components, and b) advise Chairs.

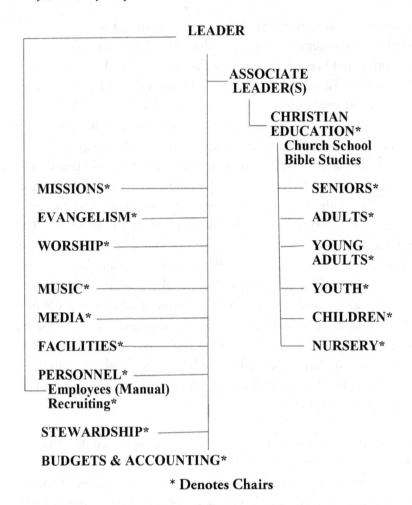

LEADER

ASSOCIATE LEADER(S)

CHRISTIAN EDUCATION*
Church School
Bible Studies

MISSIONS*

EVANGELISM*

WORSHIP*

MUSIC*

MEDIA*

FACILITIES*

PERSONNEL*
Employees (Manual)
Recruiting*

STEWARDSHIP*

BUDGETS & ACCOUNTING*

SENIORS*

ADULTS*

YOUNG ADULTS*

YOUTH*

CHILDREN*

NURSERY*

* Denotes Chairs

Figure 1 – EXAMPLE: ORGANIZATIONAL STRUCTURE

Each Chair should have its own task and its own budget to accomplish the task. For example, one Chair should not have control of all or part of the budget of another Chair. The Budgets & Accounting Chair should have final approval of the entire budget. Each Chair has to assume responsibility for contributing to the success not only of a Component but also for the success of the entire Board by providing guidance or constructive criticism of each other Chair's plan and performance to plan. **APPENDIX C** – Example of Chair Critique- There will be cases where one or more tasks will be common to more than one Chair. An example of this task is shown in **APPENDIX B** – Hosting. Unless the Board assumes such responsibility, it is possible that any of its Components could perform poorly and even become totally ineffective.

Implementation of the guidelines in this book will occur slowly and leadership must be dedicated and persistent. Leadership also will need to do a lot of training. Patience is required as well as continued FOLLOW THROUGH. Satisfactory results will be forthcoming.

Capable personnel and good management should <u>inherently</u> <u>perform</u> each of the following which are crucial to successful performance of the Board:

1. Complete the Management Course either in Seminary or in church; if not, plan to take the course.
2. Prepare the Board's plan including Component missions
3. Recruit Chairs
4. Prepare Component plan; Refer to APPENDIX D –Planning, and APPENDIX H – Youth Operating Plan Example
5. Assume responsibility for own Component and critique and contribute to each other Component plan and performance.
6. Review and approve Component budget
7. Accept constructive contribution to the plan by other Component Chairs
8. Recruit/staff Component; Refer to APPENDIX F – Staffing
9. Train staff
10. Equip Component with appropriate equipment and/or supplies
11. Make assignments within the Component
12. Each Component staff assumes responsibility to perform tasks
13. Chair assess Component performance
14. Chair takes corrective action
15. Prepare report of performance or evaluation of progress versus plan
16. Maintain a <u>composite</u> Board report that is provided to the Congregation. The Congregation will be: a) informed as to what the Board is doing, and b) effectively training them-selves. This

report could develop the church culture of having emphasis of efficiently and effectively carrying out the church mission.

17. Recognition of the part that prayer and The Holy Spirit play in guiding the Board and its Components in their contribution to the church.

18. In summary, capable personnel and appropriate management along with guidance from The Holy Spirit spells success.

CHAPTER 4 – PSYCHOLOGY OF MANAGEMENT

MESSAGE TO CHURCH LEADERS
What are your preconceptions?
Do you have capability to change?
Are you open to changes?
Will your preconceptions stand in the way of improving
the efficiency and effectiveness of the church?

Instead of doubting everything that can be doubted, let us
rather doub.t nothing until we are compelled to doubt.

Introduction of 'management' to church members can be a 'foreign' experience even for the Board's Leader and its Chairs. The Leader of the Board, based on his/her education, will need to appropriately introduce management and provide training.

Change or implementation of relatively big and new ideas is very difficult or near impossible for someone who has managed with virtually no change for years and sincerely feels there is no reason to change. In other words "it's not worth it". It is recognized that: a) virtually all people are different for one reason or another, and as a result words have different meanings to different people, and b) churches are of different sizes, cultures, intellect, social status, and consist of all ages. All of this emphasizes the need for training to somehow get everyone to a similar positive thinking level. Start by training the Board's Leader, followed by training the Chairs, or train both simultaneously. It is a fact that best communication takes place when the communication is between those who are alike. Training must precede implementation. Implementation must be done slowly depending on the degree of training.

Recruiting is one of the most important tasks to be performed. Refer to APPENDIX F – Staffing. Knowledge of the congregation and the 'personal touch' must be emphasized. Recruiting is a continual task needed, not just a one-time per year. The objectives of recruiting volunteers are: a) learn and document the congregation capabilities, b) have a list of tasks to be performed and their job descriptions, c) identify prospects, d) assess the prospects capabilities, e) match the prospects capabilities to the task to be assigned, and f) get a commitment from the prospect.

An approach to recruiting that can be successful includes the following:

- Establish a <u>permanent</u> Recruiting Committee that is active year around to perform all recruiting requirements
- Prepare a recruiting plan
- Prepare a job description for the Recruiting Committee
- Prepare the Leader's job description and job descriptions of each Chair

- Board to submit both the plans and job descriptions from each Chair to the Recruiting Committee
- Proceed to recruit each Chair's staff in coordination with each Chair

The following is an example of how many churches recruit. This is how **NOT** to recruit…..

EXAMPLE – Some recruiting committees are temporary in nature, and disbanded after recruiting either or both the Leader and Chairs. The recruiting committee recruits only the Leader and the Chairs. It does not recruit personnel to staff the Chairs' Components. The Chairs, when recruited, are not aware of the task they are to perform; the Leader assigns each recruit to a task after they are recruited. The recruiting committees receive recommendations and conduct brief interviews. In most cases a new prospect passes the interview based on personality and desire to serve. There is no <u>written</u> job description of the job to which they ultimately are assigned, and there is no <u>written</u> plan for the task to be accomplished. Also, there is little to no <u>written</u> information about what was previously accomplished. These new leaders are placed in individual leadership positions without knowing what is to be done. In some cases there is an overall understanding based on the title of the position and possibly an overall paragraph describing his/her Component. This newly recruited person must somehow gather enough knowledge to begin doing 'something' that is considered to be the task.

CHAPTER 5 – ASSUMPTION OF RESPONSIBILITY

MESSAGE TO CHURCH LEADERS
What are your preconceptions?
Do you have capability to change?
Are you open to changes?
Will your preconceptions stand in the way of improving
the efficiency and effectiveness of the church?

Instead of doubting everything that can be doubted, let us
rather doubt nothing until we are compelled to doubt.

A prerequisite to 'assumption of responsibility' is a clear definition of the task to be performed. The task to be performed is included in a 'plan'; a brief mission statement is not considered enough detail. There must be enough detail for the church leaders to identify the individual tasks that can be both assigned to and performed by individuals. Refer to APPENDIX D – Planning. Refer to Chapter 3 – Organizational Structure & Mechanical Management.

Assumption of responsibility implies 'running with the ball'; requiring minimum direction. In cases where the Chair(s) have relatively little experience, the Leader must provide training and follow-up help. In addition to plan preparation followed by personnel assignment, the Leader must involve him-self/her-self enough to clearly understand whether or not and to what extent the one to whom the task is assigned understands the plan and how to implement the plan. At this point the Leader or Chair who made the assignment should be able to detect the capability of the assignee.

Again, all involved, the Leader and each Chair must assume responsibility for performing its task and at the same time contribute to the preparation and performance to plan of each other Chair.

MEETINGS

There should be at least five kinds of meetings with emphasis on involvement by everyone. Each meeting should be a pleasant experience with the common interest and satisfaction of serving God.

1. Pastor's staff meeting
2. Board meeting (once a month)
   a. Management training (Include Organization Chart)
   b. Adopt 'Guidelines for Management' as permanent policy
   c. Review the Board's plan including critiques. This is effectively the plan for the entire church which includes how the church is going to implement elements of the Seminaries' mission statements.
   d. Review each Chair's plan including critiques and revised plans
   e. Review each Chair's performance to plan

3. Leader's meetings with each Chair individually
   a. Assist Chair in preparing plan
   b. Review performance to plan
4. Chair meetings with Chair's staff
   a. Review and critique plan
   b. Discuss assignments & review performance to plan
5. Leader's meeting with individual congregation members. This effectively can advocate the Pastor's 'open door' policy.

SUMMARY GUIDELINES FOR MANAGEMENT

POLICY STATEMENT – The Board should pass a POLICY STATEMENT motion that establishes these guidelines as permanent policy. This policy statement should include that the Leader must use these guidelines in conducting EACH Board meeting.

LEADER – The Leader: a) should have either completed the seminary 'management course' while in seminary, or b) plans to take the seminary 'management course' at a seminar provided by a seminary, c) should provide direction to each Chair and support the Chair in providing direction to the staff of each Chair.

CHAIR – Each Chair should prepare and implement his/her own plan and must critique each other Chair's plan.

RECRUITING COMPONENT – This COMPONENT must be active year around and: a) recruit all church positions including Leader, Associate Leader, Chairs, and staff of Chairs, and b) conduct individual training sessions for the Board and congregation.

PLAN – The Leader and each Chair should individually prepare a plan listing tasks to be accomplished and how the tasks are to be accomplished. Include staffing requirements.

MEETINGS – The Leader should: a) conduct the Board meetings, b) meet with each Chair individually to assist the Chair in plan preparation, and c) discuss status.

BUDGET – Individual budgets should be allocated to the Leader and each Chair.

CHAPTER 6 – RECOMMENDATIONS

MESSAGE TO CHURCH LEADERS
What are your preconceptions?
Do you have capability to change?
Are you open to changes?
Will your preconceptions stand in the way of improving
the efficiency and effectiveness of the church?

Instead of doubting everything that can be doubted, let us
rather doubt nothing until we are compelled to doubt.

The following recommendations are provided:

1. The organization above Seminaries should prepare a master plan for each Seminary to include a management course in their curriculum that includes: leadership, planning, organizing, staffing, motivating, and controlling.
2. The organization above Seminaries or each Seminary should prepare a management course that includes: leadership, planning, organizing, staffing, motivating, and controlling.
3. Include in the management course the preparation of plans to accomplish: a) Seminaries' mission statement objectives, b) Board objectives, and c) Component objectives.
4. The management course should be taught: a) on Seminary campus and satellites, and b) in churches and satellites for those Pastors and Lay leaders who have not had the opportunity to take the course.
5. Seminaries should pursue individual churches in offering to conduct the management course in their church.

APPENDIX A – MEDIA MINISTRIES OPERATING PLAN

NOTE: Portions of this plan have been redacted to avoid identifying the specific church at which this plan was used. The redacted book location is identified by brackets, thusly, [].

PURPOSE – This plan is used to document and manage operation of Media Ministries. This plan is available to anyone who is interested in: a) understanding the organization, b) evaluating performance, and c) identifying potential improvements.

MISSION: The mission is to multiply the number of individuals, both local and global, who hear sermons, participate in Bible study, pursue knowledge of church activities, and pursue a personal relationship with Jesus Christ. This mission is achieved by utilization of sound, light, projection, and video recordings of Worship Services and Bible Studies to capture videos which are uploaded to vimeo.com for viewing (playing).

STATISTICS: Vimeo.com provided the following statistics covering five and one half years beginning March 2009 and ending October 1, 2014:

Total Plays   11,628
Plays per Month   174
Plays per Week   43

This is equivalent to a Bible Study class running 52 weeks per year for five (5) years with 43 attending every week.

INTRODUCTION –The Recording Ministry was established in memory of [] in 2007 and is privately financed. The original missions were to video record Worship Services and create DVDs for those who could not attend Worship Services for various reasons. At that time the name, Recording Ministry, was appropriate. Since then the Recording Ministry has significantly expanded its assumption of responsibility to include not only Video Recording and DVD creation, duplication, and distribution, but also:

- Sound
- Theatrical Lighting
- Video Recording, Processing, and Original Creation

- Computer Projection-Video & Sound
- Assisted Listening
- Still Photography
- DVD Cover Design, Duplication & Distribution
- Audio/Video Cart
- Support of Church Activities
- Video Broadcasting-Real Time Streaming Video (TBD)

Therefore, the name, Recording Ministry, was changed to Media Ministries; to be better representative.

Media Ministries reports to [].

Media Ministries facilities include: [].

MISSION – Enhance Worship Services and Pastor's Bible Study. Multiply the number of individuals, both local and global, who hear/view sermons, participate in Bible study, pursue knowledge of church activities, and pursue a personal relationship with Jesus Christ. Support Café Worship as required. Support various church organizations, functions at the church, and enable use of audio and video.

CREDIT – Our life is the life of Christ, mediated in us by the indwelling Holy Spirit. The more constant our communication with the indwelling Christ, the better we are pruned and the more fruit we are able to produce. Any accomplishments of ours are due to Christ, not to our own effort. Colossians 3:17 – [17] And whatever you do, whether in word or deed, do it all in the name of the Lord Jesus, giving thanks to God the Father through him.

Remember, you are working for God, not individuals.

STAFFING – The following staffing is provided on a weekly basis:

- 1 ea. – Sanctuary preparation for events
- 1 ea. – Video camera recording (One Worship Service)
- 1 ea. – Sound/mixer operation (Two Worship Services)

- 1 ea. – Projection (Two Worship Services)
- 1 ea. – Lighting control (Two Worship Services)
- 1 ea. – Video download from camera recording to computer, then upload to vimeo.com
- 1 ea. – Video editing of Worship Service video, then upload to vimeo.com
- 2 ea. – Daybreak Bible Study (video recording, mixer operation, projection)
- 1 ea. – Personnel Assignments (Sound/mixer, Projection, Lighting, Camera operation)

Staffing also is provided for special events such as the following including rehearsals:

- Piano Recital
- Organ Recital
- Children's Choir Musical
- Children's Christmas Eve Program
- Vacation Bible School
- [] Summer Concert
- Christmas Concert
- Others

Staffing also is provided during the week to support requests from the church staff and others within the church.

TECHNICAL TASKS – Including:

- Assure appropriate setup of sound in the Sanctuary and Chapel for events.
- Maintain the technical portion of the Media Ministries Manual.
- Interface, when necessary, with [].
- Perform Reverberation Time tests in the Sanctuary when deemed necessary
- Calibrate/adjust Digital Signal Processor when deemed necessary
- Battery management; assure charged batteries are available as needed and installed in appropriate equipment including both

the wireless mics used in the Sanctuary and the Assisted Listening receivers.

- Video recording is performed using a Sony Solid-State Memory Camcorder PMW-EX-1 mounted on a Manfrotto fluid mount tripod.
- Running sound is performed by use of inputs from microphones and media playback devices to Yamaha L9-32 Digital Mixer.
- Projection is accomplished by laptop computer input to two Mitsubishi DLP XD8100U projectors and one Panasonic PT-VX400NT projector – two for the Congregation and one for the Chancel.
- Align the two images projected from the Mitsubishi projectors when necessary.
- Lighting control of twelve theatrical lights is performed using a laptop computer with LightFactory software controlling lights via DMX communication protocol involving four Chauvet PRO-6 Dimmer Relay Racks
- Video processing is performed using Sony Vegas Pro 12 software installed on three desktop computers linked together on one Network Drive.
- DVDs are duplicated using a Sony Duplicator which duplicates seven disks 'simultaneously'.
- DVD covers are designed and printed directly on the disk using Epson Print CD software.
- DVDs are distributed weekly to those unable to attend Worship Services.
- Still photography produces photos edited with Photoshop software for documentation and communication purposes.
- Prepare PowerPoint presentations.
- Perform equipment and software maintenance and upgrade.
- Provide training for personnel.
- Provide support to the [] Worship Service.

ADMINSTRATIVE TASKS – Administrative tasks include:

- Prepare and maintain current the Administration portion of the Media Ministries Manual.
- Schedule and assign personnel weekly to operate camera, mixer, computer for projection, and lighting control computer for each event.
- Distribute DVDs.
- Provide safe storage of master disks for backup and duplication.
- Recruit and train personnel.
- Provide maintenance for computers and peripherals
- Procure computer and camera equipment and office supplies.
- Report activities to Business Administrator.
- Maintain current the Assisted Listening Ear Bud assignment 'board'.
- Prepare articles for Worship Service Bulletin and Spire.
- Analyze Vimeo media statistics and produce reports.
- Provide physical storage with ready access for video sound, and lighting equipment.
- Procure Vimeo storage periodically as additional storage is needed.
- Provide audio/video cart for church personnel usage.

APPENDIX B — HOSTING GUIDELINES

This is a very rough draft. [] have experienced guests arriving at the church having no contact; just floating around. [] have experienced 'last minute' need for a host.

At least three areas have guests/visitors to the church of various types and should host these guests. These areas include:

- ➤ Pastor(s)
- ➤ Mission Component
- ➤ Worship and Music Component

The Pastor has guests/visitors to the church that fall into two categories: a) more personal guests he/she prefers hosting, and b) guests he/she would expect the Worship Component host.

Guests from, for example, the [] should be hosted by the Mission Component. Guest musicians and guest choirs, both children and adults, for example, should be hosted by the Music Component. Guests of Pastor(s) not hosted by Pastor(s) should be hosted by the Worship Component. Hosting is a very important task and can at times be very involved.

CASE FOR MISSION COMPONENT (See Chapter 2 Organization Structure)

Example No. 1: Guest arriving via airline, has no transportation, and needs lodging.

- ➤ Identify Host and get commitment that he/she will be responsible for the guest from arrival to departure. In case the committee chair cannot perform the task of the host, it is the responsibility of this chair to identify a host within his/her committee and 'train' the 'substitute' in details such as those noted below. In some cases it might be necessary for the chair to cancel previous personal plans and perform the task of host.

➤ Name of Host
➤ Name of Guest
➤ Airline
➤ Arrival time
➤ Departure time
➤ Meet guest at airport
➤ Transport guest during entire visit
➤ Accommodate any special needs of the guest, and there can be one or more.
➤ Provide lodging (first night)
➤ Provide breakfast
➤ Transport guest to church
➤ Introduce guest to many members
➤ Arrange for guest to meet with group(s)
➤ Make reservations for lunch
➤ Invite specific members, not the entire church, to attend luncheon
➤ Attend luncheon and pay guests tab
➤ Tour guest over the city to previously planned sites
➤ Provide a resting place like for the remainder of the afternoon in the Host's home
➤ Take guest to dinner
➤ Provide lodging (last night)
➤ Take guest to airport for departure
➤ Others not included above

In case the Host is assisted by one or more individuals, all individuals involved need to know the specific hour when and where the exchange is to take place, not just in the morning or afternoon.

CASE FOR MUSIC COMPONENT (See Chapter 2 Organization Structure)

Example No. 2:

Two groups are performing and **we need a single host to be in charge of this**, are: 1) [], and 2) []. These groups already have accommodations. Needs exist for guides here on church campus doing the following:

> ➤ Check singers in and tell them where to go (pass out little maps of our campus)
> ➤ Attend to needs of directors: last minute things. All set-up needs should be prepared in advance: tables, chairs, computer needs, projectors, sound, heat, music stands, water, coffee, tissues, pencils, welcome signs or specific directional sign, etc. Someone should be responsible for double checking all of that before anyone arrives.
> ➤ Managing the schedule and facilitating movement of groups to their assigned rooms, etc. during this festival, there are three to four groups who rehearse at the same time at various locations and then need to move to rehearse together with other groups - we are talking about moving 150-200 children all at once! We should have a guide assigned to each group who knows the campus and can assist with any needs that arise for that group. Children can get sick, have to use the bathroom, pass out, start crying and feeling homesick, etc. during rehearsal.

This particular event needs a team of people with **one person in charge**, being the host, to manage this task so everything goes smoothly. [] is meeting with the event organizers on [], and it would be most desirable for this host attend this meeting with me.

APPENDIX C – EXAMPLE OF CHAIR CRITIQUE

The Chair has done a very good job; however, there are some recommended additions, deletions, and changes to the Chair's plan.

It is recommended that the following be added:
1.
2.
3.
Etc.

It is recommended that the following be deleted:
1.
2.
3.
Etc.

It is recommended that the following be changed:
1.
2.
3.
Etc.

It is recommended that the following tasks be moved from this Chair to another Chair.

The staffing will need to be revised to incorporate the above.

APPENDIX D - PLANNING

The Leader should inform all Chairs that he/she is vitally interested in having each Chair prepare a plan for their organization, and that the Leader wants to help each Chair <u>individually</u>. This participation is proof to the Chairs that the Leader is most interested in each of them and wants each Chair to be a good manager and contribute to the successful performance of the church. This provides leadership development and development of the Chairs' spiritual gifts.

A plan is a list of objectives, and <u>can</u> contain descriptions of the objectives in <u>both</u> broad and detailed terms. It <u>can</u> include procedures as to how to achieve the objectives. It <u>can</u> include staffing requirements to achieve the objectives. In businesses there are tactical and strategic plans; tactical meaning near term and strategic meaning long term.

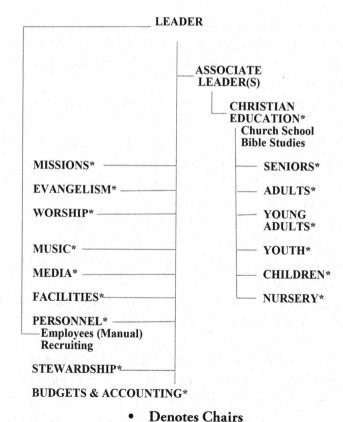

LEADER

ASSOCIATE LEADER(S)

CHRISTIAN EDUCATION*
Church School
Bible Studies

MISSIONS*   — SENIORS*

EVANGELISM*   — ADULTS*

WORSHIP*   — YOUNG ADULTS*

MUSIC*   — YOUTH*

MEDIA*   — CHILDREN*

FACILITIES*   — NURSERY*

PERSONNEL*
Employees (Manual)
Recruiting

STEWARDSHIP*

BUDGETS & ACCOUNTING*

• **Denotes Chairs**

Figure 1 – ORGANIZATIONAL STRUCTURE

It appears obvious that every church should have and most likely does have plans. However, because of the nature of the relational management philosophy and business as usual used by Leaders in the church, the plan is not prepared and used as it should be. Leaders in the church have different experiences from those who have successfully used the hierarchical management philosophy. Most Leaders in the church have no experience in managing an organization firmly grounded in getting tasks accomplished thru use of in-depth basic management functions. There is a sense that virtually no direction should be provided. There is a lack of understanding of the meaning of direction. It appears to leadership in the church that 'direction' comes from a dictator type of personality which should not be used when the Board consists of mostly volunteers. This understanding can so permeate the organization that:

- A plan for each Chair does not exist.
- There is no adequate documentation of previous performance.
- There is no transition of leadership because little to no documentation exists.
- Chairs are appointed as Chairs without properly matching capability to task.
- Chairs are assigned poorly defined tasks for which it is assumed they will assume responsibility.
- Chairs vary in capability from capable to very little capability.
- Little to no direction is provided to Chairs.
- Lack of direction produces minimal results.
- Lack of **Leader** involvement in Chair task performance results in lack of in-depth knowledge of the status of the task and possible knowledge of the task itself.
- Chairs have no budgets, and as a result are not involved in performing to budget or forecasting to budget.

When there is no plan, it is very common in the church that every year, without question, newly recruited Chairs say: "What am I supposed to do; am I supposed to reinvent the wheel; there is no plan for my 'Component' or committee; what was done during the previous year(s); what am I to do now?" Yes, this is sad especially when only a mission statement exists for the Chairs. Without an operating plan, there is little to no effective transition.

CAUTION – It is not enough to have a plan without some detail as to how to implement the plan. For example, the following are good objectives, but detail must exist as to how to achieve the objectives:

- Experience Jesus
- Strengthen Christ's Church
- Journey Into Deeper Faith
- Transform Our World

It is not enough to just 'tack on' the above labels to existing activities without a written plan to accomplish these 'objectives'. Without a plan and without follow up, it is doubtful that the good objectives will ever be achieved.

A plan is a 'working' document. It is prepared for several reasons, some of which are it:

- Communicates to others that the Board not only is in name only, but the Board is well managed
- Organizes the Chair's thoughts
- Identifies tasks that can be assigned to the Chair's staff
- The Chair's staff know what they are to do
- Is a reference for reporting
- Tells others what the Chair plans to do
- Provides others with the opportunity to contribute to its content
- Is a major aid in transitioning the task to others
- Is an aid in training Chairs to manage

Preparing a plan does require <u>thought</u>, and it does require someone to <u>write</u>. A Chair without proper management experience can say: "We really don't need this." This is a 'business as usual do nothing attitude', and is the 'easy way out', and limits the entire church contribution, and especially individual contribution and appreciation of the church. All that needs to be done is to <u>ask</u> someone, even without experience, to prepare a plan and provide as much help as practical. **APPENDIX H – Youth Operating**

Plan Example is a very rough example of tasks that might be included in a "Youth Operating Plan".

With assistance from the Leader, one Chair who has never prepared a plan can start preparation of a plan that consists of possibly very few tasks. Then, the needed staff is identified; they are recruited; the recruited personnel begin to see results; an esprit de corps develops; and the Chair begins to appreciate the results. The Chair might even add tasks to the plan. The almost non-existent organization grows. The entire church begins to see and appreciate the results and the personality of the church changes for the better especially when each of the Chairs does the same. This does require dedicated and capable leadership including especially follow through.

Not only will the leadership be motivated, but the entire congregation would be motivated when leadership is 'open' and communicates fully with the congregation. The congregation could communicate its desires for including items based on their personal experiences at work or in a previous church. However, the atmosphere must be such to encourage such participation. Unfortunately, without this encouragement, capable church members are relegated to just attending Worship Services and maybe a Bible Study, and then go home. This is a massive loss in contribution.

BUDGET

Budget is part of the plan. The Leader and each Chair should have its own task and its own budget to accomplish the task. For example, one Chair should not have control of all or part of the budget of another Chair. The Budgets & Accounting Chair should have final approval of the entire budget and authority to make revisions to the budget as required. Plans must be the basis of allocating budgets and as such, performance to budget is the task of each Chair. Since the task of some Chairs will be performed entirely by volunteers, there is no need for a budget for all Chairs. There should be a one-to-one relationship between the task(s) to be performed and the budgets for the task(s) to be performed. In turn, the Chair could provide budget forecasts.

APPENDIX E – REJECTED OPERATING PLAN PROPOSAL

NOTE: This was a presentation to Leadership resulting in a lack of acceptance. The proposal just 'died'. The term 'committee' is used here since the church for which this was presented uses the term committee instead of component used in this book.

PURPOSE
OF
OPERATING PLAN

Provide basis for:

- **More complete definition of task to be performed**
- **Greater participation by Leaders in Committee Operation**
- **Improved communication with:**
- ✓ **Committees**
- ✓ **Congregation**
- **Improved Committee performance**
- **Specific constructive criticism**
- **New Leader orientation**
- **Continuity**
- **Mission re-evaluation**

CURRENT SITUATION
Leadership relative to Committees

Leadership Participation
- Brief monthly reports/statements

Leadership communication
- Listen to monthly reports/statements
- Virtually no feedback to committees

Leadership contribution to performance
- Relatively none

Leadership constructive criticism
- Relatively none

Committee performance improvement
- Little incentive

New Leader orientation
- None in most cases

Continuity
- Word of mouth
- Dependent on characteristics of assigned Leader

Re-evaluate mission
- None

RESULT

Entire operation is STATUS QUO with some exceptions:
- **Routine matters**
- **Special occasions**
- **Problems encountered**

NO FIX
OR
FIX

- Continue status quo
- Assume Leadership responsibility and fix the problem

EXPECTATIONS

Each Chair read/study submitted Operating Plan

Recommend additions/deletions/revisions in form of:
- Written book and/or
- Mark-up of Operating Plan

Chairs:
- Incorporate additions/deletions/revisions as deemed necessary
- Provide feedback to source of critique

RECOMMENDATION

I move that:

1) The Board approve that each Chair prepare its own Operating Plan, and

2) An ADHOC committee be appointed to implement preparation and use of each Chair Operating Plan.

APPENDIX F – STAFFING

Staffing requirements are determined by the structure of the organization and the plans prepared by the Chairs. The structure identifies the Leader, Associate Leaders, and the Chairs, and the Chairs' prepare plans that identify their personnel requirements to staff their plans. In all cases, job descriptions describe the tasks to be accomplished.

Recruiting is one of the most important tasks to be performed. Advertising should be used; however, knowledge of the congregation and the 'personal touch' should be emphasized.

Recruiting requires a 'personal touch'. Recruiting is a continual task needed to replace attrition.

The objective of recruiting volunteers is to identify and get a commitment from a prospective person or recruit to staff a job that this person can perform successfully. This requires the recruiter to match the person's capability with the job description. Some jobs would require stronger spiritual gifts than others. The job description can be very brief; it does not have to be complex.

An approach to recruiting that has been successful includes the following:

- Establish a permanent Recruiting Committee that is active year around to perform all recruiting requirements
- Prepare a recruiting plan
- Prepare a job description for the Recruiting Committee
- Prepare the Leader's job description and job descriptions of each Chair
- Board to submit both the plans and job descriptions from each Chair to the Recruiting Committee
- Proceed to staff each Chair's organization in coordination with each Chair

The following is an example of how many churches recruit. This is how not to recruit…..

EXAMPLE – Most recruiting committees are temporary in nature, and disbanded after recruiting either or both the Leader and Chairs. The Chairs, when recruited, are not aware of the task they are to perform; the Leader assigns each recruit to a task after they are recruited. The recruiting committees receive recommendations and conduct brief interviews. In most cases a new prospect passes the interview based on personality and desire to serve. There is no <u>written</u> job description of the job to which they ultimately are assigned, and there is no <u>written</u> plan for the task to be accomplished. Also, there is little to no <u>written</u> information about what was previously accomplished. These new leaders are placed in individual leadership positions without knowing what is to be done. In some cases there is an overall understanding based on the title of the position and possibly an overall paragraph describing his/her organization. This newly recruited person must somehow gather enough knowledge to begin doing 'something' that is considered to be the task.

It should be noted that once the organizational structure is in place, and plans are prepared and each Chair has staffed their Component, the organization, the plans, and the staffing can remain in place almost indefinitely. Plans most likely will be revised periodically and staff attrition will require some periodic recruiting.

APPENDIX G – MOTIVATING & CONTROLLING

The Leader's 'human touch' is so important in motivating and controlling. The Leader must not be a dictator. The Leader must be a 'friend', but at the same time possess capability recognized by everyone. The Leader should inform all Chairs that he/she is vitally interested in working with each Chair individually. A by-product of this working together is that both the Leader and Chair learn, and as a result the congregation is educated and feels that they are involved and can contribute. The entire church grows.

The atmosphere during each Board meeting and each Leader meeting with each Chair must be mutual respect between everyone on the Board and especially mutual respect between the Leader and each Chair. There should be no embarrassment, and everyone should have the attitude of wanting to help each other.

LEADER MODERATES BOARD

The routine Board agenda should include for each Chair:

- Policy statement (See Chapter 2)
- Status of plan preparation
- Identification of each task included in the plan
- Identification of current active and potentially active tasks
- Staffing status including job description of Chair and job description of staff
- Current task activity status
- Budget status
- Request for Chair critiques, suggestions, and evaluations; recommended additions, deletions, and modifications

There is no place for trying to make the meeting 'short'. This does not imply that inefficiency is acceptable. The emphasis should be on 'getting the job done'. The Leader and Chairs should have the desire to produce the best plans feasible, and implement these plans effectively.

LEADER MEETING WITH CHAIR

The routine agenda should include essentially the same elements as included in the Board meeting:

- Status of plan preparation
- Identification of each task included in the plan
- Identification of current active and potentially active tasks
- Staffing status including job description of Chair and job description of staff
- Current task activity status
- Budget status
- Request for Chair critiques; recommended additions, deletions, and modifications

CAUTION – FOLLOW THROUGH

Implementation of the organizational structure included in Chapter 2 and the meeting approach noted above can take a relatively long time for everyone to feel comfortable, so patience is required as well as continued FOLLOW THROUGH. Satisfactory results will be forthcoming.

BUSINESS AS USUAL VS IN-DEPTH USE OF BASIC FUNCTIONS OF MANAGEMENT

Many churches use the 'business as usual' management philosophy with extremely limited applications of the basic functions of management. This limited use of these functions produces limited results, and in some cases no results. These functions are in business textbooks to provide managers the way to successfully achieve high performance yielding much desired results. Churches should avoid the 'business as usual' philosophy especially when there are proven management philosophies that produce high performance with much better results.

Leaders who use the 'business as usual' concept, continue down the same path as always and are quite satisfied with current performance, and see no reason to change. The 'business as usual' management philosophy provides no improvement. Their 'minds are made up' and little interest exists in improvement. See **APPENDIX E** – Rejected Operating Plan Proposal that was rejected. The mind must be <u>honestly</u> open and seek new ideas. **'Business as usual' has been used for years and getting leadership to change even for improvement is very difficult and, unfortunately, sometimes impossible.** Basic business functions, when properly understood and applied while working together provide a synergistic result that produces the end result which is the objective of effectively managing programs in the church.

RELATIONAL MANAGEMENT PHILOSOPHY

The church can be referred to as a 'relational' organization because it dominantly consists of volunteers in contrast to paid personnel. To some, this implies providing very little detailed Leader involvement resulting in providing virtually no direction. Providing direction as in the hierarchical organization is considered dictatorial in nature by 'relational' leaders. Hierarchical management really is relational with one exception, and that is the Leader has the unchallenged authority to make decisions and provide direction. This is not considered dictatorial. It is considered 'good business practice'. Making decisions, and providing direction, must be done in an acceptable manner to achieve desired results. There is no place for a dictator, and **the dictator will have difficulty surviving.**

BUSINESS AS USUAL RESPONSE TO CHANGE

The 'business as usual' management philosophy provides no improvement. Their 'minds are made up' and little interest exists in improvement. The mind must be <u>honestly</u> open and seek new ideas.

When attempts are being made to get the "business as usual" leader to implement change, there can appear that progress to change is being made; however, you will not know until changes are really made.

The following are some of the characteristics most likely present:

- Inherently 'business as usual' – no change
- Perceived barriers – no available funds; can't afford it; no change in overall budget structure
- Mutual respect – perceived barriers over shadow mutual respect
- Sincerity – questionable
- Tolerance – tolerance without change; delay tactics
- Desire to understand new ideas – questionable
- Capability to understand new ideas – questionable

APPENDIX H – YOUTH OPERATING PLAN EXAMPLE

NOTE: <u>This plan is only a rough guide</u>. Initial preparation can start with much less contend and be improved as progress is made. Staffing is a prime consideration.

PURPOSE

The purpose of this plan is to: communicate with both Leadership and the congregation.
Some of the items that could be included in the plan are:

1. Christian education
2. Spiritual fellowship
3. Family Christian growth
4. Entertainment
5. Worship opportunities
6. Outreach to non-churched youth and their families;
7. Parent development and adult counselors and sponsors.
8. Development of a young ministry leadership team;
9. Opportunities for Youth to get exposure and participate in as many church adult Component activities as practical.

DATABASE

Build and maintain a database to include the following:

- Youth in church-member households
- Youth in church non-member households
- Records of:
✓ Attendance
✓ Event participation
✓ Individual contacts to encourage Youth in church non-member households to become active in the Youth ministry
- Prepare reports of the above

1. CHRISTIAN EDUCATION

Provide Christian education using a Christian Education curriculum in classroom environment for K-7 through K-12 during the public school year. An example of the curriculum is as follows:

[Include example]

2. SPIRITUAL FELLOWSHIP

- Provide activities on campus and off campus.
- Integrate Youth into as many adult organizations as practical (A parent could/should accompany the youth.)

3. CHRISTIAN ENTERTAINMENT

Provide Christian entertainment in a variety of forms on church campus and off-site.

[Expand to include details.]

4. FAMILY GROWTH

Integrate Youth into as many adult organizations as practical (Encourage parent(s) to accompany the youth.)

[Expand to include details]

5. WORSHIP

Provide Youth Worship Services following a specific agenda each Sunday following Christian Education classes. The agenda should include elements of Service provided in the Main Sanctuary.

[Expand to include details]

6. OUTREACH TO NON-CHURCHED YOUTH AND THEIR FAMILIES

Use the database noted under Christian Education above.

[Expand to include details]

7. MISSION OUTREACH

[Expand to include details]

8. PARENT AND ADULD COUNSELORS AND SPONSORS

[Expand to include details]

9. YOUNG MINISTRY LEADERSHIP TEAM

[Expand to include details]

10. COMMITMENT TO CHRISTIAN SERVICE

[Expand to include details]

11. PARTICIPATION IN EACH LEDERSHIP COMPONENT ACTIVITY

[Expand to include details]

12. PARTICIPATION IN PREPARATION OF DATA FOR INCLUSION ON CHURCH WEBSITE

[Expand to include details]

APPENDIX I - MEDIA MINISTRIES HISTORY

NOTE: Portions of this Media Ministries operating plan included in **APPENDIX I** have been redacted to avoid identifying the specific church at which this plan was used. The redacted book location is identified by brackets, thusly, [].

Media Ministries was established in memory of [] in 2007 and was privately financed and voluntarily managed until January 1, 2015. The tasks performed by Media Ministries include:

- Sound
- Theatrical Lighting
- Video Recording, Processing, and Original Creation
- Computer Projection-Video & Sound
- Assisted Listening
- Still Photography
- DVD Cover Design, Duplication & Distribution
- Audio/Video Mobile Cart
- Support of Church Activities
- Uploading videos of Worship Services, Sermons, Bible Studies, and Special Events to vimeo.com for global access

Twenty-five or more volunteer personnel with desire and capability were recruited at any one time. The video recordings are stored on the website vimeo.com where access to each video was available globally. The global ministry provided videos that were 'completely played' on vimeo.com, not just accessed, in over 120 countries. Examples of the videos are as follows:

Bible Studies:
    World Religions
    Cults
    Ten (10) books of the Bible
Sermons:
    Thirty-nine (39) books of the Bible
Special Events:
    Piano Concerts
    Organ Concerts

Band Concerts
Christmas Concerts
Easter Concerts
Complete Worship Services
Numerous

It was realized that at some point in time the church would have to assume total responsibility for Media Ministries. So, the church decided to assume responsibility for and manage Media Ministries beginning January 1, 2015. The transition was rough. The global ministry was destroyed by eliminating use of vimeo.com, and the local ministry was significantly limited to: a) supporting worship services, and b) video recording only sermons <u>without</u> <u>editing</u> for uploading to the church website only. Many of the tasks included in the Operating Plan such as lighting, etc. were either eliminated or ignored. **The result of what happened reveals the need to implement significant management changes.**

THE TRANSITION

The author has participated in numerous transitions in for-profit business as well as the church. These transitions were of two types: a) accepting new tasks <u>from</u> others, and b) transferring tasks <u>to</u> others. In all cases there was a mutual understanding and, most of all, acceptance of the tasks as originally defined. In the Media Ministries case, there was little exchange of information. The new leader: a) did not accept the tasks as defined, and b) lacked understanding of tasks as defined. Most of the information available was not transferred because of a lack of interest. Dominant interest became 'sound' with lesser and in some cases no interest in the other tasks. Problems were created by proceeding to make unilateral changes resulting in poor performance. When problems occurred in performing tasks, attempts were made to solve the problems; however, ultimately the tasks were eliminated instead of fixing the problem. Staffing needs were decreased by eliminating tasks, and little effort was spent on recruiting.

Media Ministries was destroyed as a result of poor management, namely 'business as usual' along with use of the relational management technique. This technique allowed Leadership to:

- Have no operating plan
- Provide virtually no direction to participants,
- Have a lack of desire to provide direction,
- Have a lack of desire to participate, thereby limiting their knowledge of the tasks,
- Have a limited understanding and or appreciation of the total scope of the task, and
- Destroy what many churches work so hard to accomplish.

This kind of thing should never be allowed to happen in any organization.

The following is a list of folders in which videos were included. These were removed (deleted/destroyed) from vimeo.com. In addition to this list are Worship Service and Special Event videos.

BIBLE STUDY

A_BIBLE STUDY_THE STORY   B_Bible Study – Galatians
B_Bible Study – John 1, 2, 3   B_Bible Study – John
B_Bible Study – Acts   B_Bible Study – Philippians
B_Bible Study – Colossians   B_Bible Study – Thessalonians 1
B_Bible Study – Corinthians   B_Bible Study – Thessalonians 2
B_Bible Study – Cults   B_Bible Study – World Religions
B_Bible Study – Ephesians

SERMONS BASED ON BOOKS OF THE BIBLE

Bible_Book – Acts
Bible_Book – Chronicles 1
Bible_Book – Colossians
Bible_Book – Corinthians 1
Bible_Book – Corinthians 2
Bible_Book – Deuteronomy
Bible_Book – Ephesians
Bible_Book – Exodus
Bible_Book – Ezekial
Bible_Book – Galatians
Bible_Book – Genesis
Bible_Book – Hebrews
Bible_Book – Isaiah
Bible_Book – James
Bible_Book – Jeremiah
Bible_Book – John 1
Bible_Book – John
Bible_Book – Luke
Bible_Book – Malachi
Bible_Book – Mark

Bible_Book – Matthew
Bible_Book – Micah
Bible_Book – Nehemiah
Bible_Book – Numbers
Bible_Book – Peter 1
Bible_Book – Philemon
Bible_Book – Phillippians
Bible_Book – Proverbs
Bible_Book – Psalms
Bible_Book – Revelation
Bible_Book – Romans
Bible_Book – Ruth
Bible_Book – Samuel 1
Bible_Book – Samuel 2
Bible_Book – Thessalonians 1
Bible_Book – Timothy 1
Bible_Book – Timothy 2
Bible_Book – Titus
Bible_Book – Zephania

ABOUT THE AUTHOR

Henry Loyd Copeland
BSEE, MS, MBA
Deacon, Elder
Founder: Media Ministries
Author: "Who Is God?" and "Church Program Management"

The author is a Christian lay person with over 40 years of engineering management experience emphasizing the basic functions of management: planning, organizing, staffing, motivating, and controlling. He also taught 'Business' at the Community College level for several years. He recognizes that personnel are one, if not, the most important ingredient in an organization. As such, he treats personnel with respect. His philosophy is to perform the existing task, and at the same time, spend time and talent to identify new tasks and new ways to perform tasks more efficiently and effectively. He has served several terms as a Leader in local churches. He is author of two books: "Who Is God?" and "Church Program Management". He has had both positive and negative experiences as a member of churches.

One negative experience motivated him to write this book. This negative experience was the virtual destruction (almost complete non-compliance with the Media Ministries Operating Plan included as APPENDIX A. Media Ministries was both a local and global ministry that he founded in 2007 and voluntarily financed and managed until January 1, 2015. This experience gave him in-depth insight as to how some churches are managed. One cannot escalate a problem to the 'top' and expect it to be resolved when the capability is not there.

FREE PREVIEW

The main purpose of this book is to achieve the objective of getting Seminaries to include a management course that includes: leadership, planning, organizing, staffing, motivating, and controlling in their curriculum. The lack of a management course in the Seminary curriculum is a very serious flaw. This book also includes valuable church program management information for church Pastors and Lay leaders.

Many churches have no 'management environment'. They are virtually 100% spiritual, and this is considered most, if not all that is desired. However, the item that is missing is application of 'management' that is taught in a 'management' course that includes: leadership, planning, organizing, staffing, motivating, and controlling.

The reader of this book who has theological education background most likely is both aware that 'leadership' is taught in seminaries, and has taken the course; however, it is apparent that 'leadership' education takes lower priority, as it should, to theological education. This is evidenced in worse case by making 'leadership' an elective. There also is an 'internship' course where the student works in a church for maybe a year at very little part time. This is where the student is to get exposure to the actual functioning of a church. Neither of these is sufficiently intense as one of the theological courses. Not only is there a lack of intensity, but also, the content of a 'leadership' course is inadequate as compared to a 'management' course that covers the basic functions of management, namely, leadership, planning, organizing, motivating, and controlling. As a result, the student upon ordination is not prepared to effectively contribute using the basic functions of management. This can result in poor performance as noted

93

in the cases included in this book. It is a fact that without effective 'management' education, a Pastor will be significantly less effective in applying theological education. This poor performance can also result in churches not having plans to accomplish what Seminaries have included, as the intent to be accomplished, in their mission statements.

'Management' can further increase effectiveness of the church's achieving its mission. The central focus of every part of the church should be building up the church spiritually and carrying the gospel to all; however, this cannot be accomplished efficiently and effectively without good management which includes leadership, planning, organizing, staffing, motivation, and controlling.

KEYNOTE

The main purpose of this book is to achieve the objective of getting Seminaries to include a management course that includes: leadership, planning, organizing, staffing, motivating, and controlling in their curriculum. The lack of a management course in the Seminary curriculum is a very serious flaw. This book also includes valuable church program management information for church Pastors and Lay leaders.

The reader of this book who has theological education background most likely is both aware that 'leadership' is taught in seminaries, and has taken the course; however, it is apparent that 'leadership' education takes lower priority, as it should, to theological education. This is evidenced in worse case by making 'leadership' an elective. There also is an 'internship' course where the student works in a church for maybe a year at very little part time. This is where the student is to get exposure to the actual functioning of a church. Neither of these is sufficiently intense as one of the theological courses. Not only is there a lack of intensity, but also, the content of a 'leadership' course is inadequate as compared to a 'management' course that covers the basic functions of management, namely, leadership, planning, organizing, staffing, motivating, and controlling. As a result, the student upon ordination is not prepared to effectively contribute using the basic functions of management. This can result in poor performance as noted in the cases included in this book. It is a fact that without effective 'management' education, a Pastor will be significantly less effective in applying theological education. This poor performance can also result in churches not having plans to accomplish what Seminaries have included, as the intent to be accomplished, in their mission statements.

A Pastor should be both a church manager as well as a spiritual leader. Without management training, it is easy to not "rock the boat" and fall into the "business as usual" pitfall. This can result in being a case of having a 'terminal disease' without knowing it. In many cases, the cause of this problem is a combination of 'business as usual', lack of 'know how', and lack of in-depth knowledge of and dependence on The Holy Spirit.

Printed in the United States
By Bookmasters